the
UNOFFICIAL
rules
of sailing

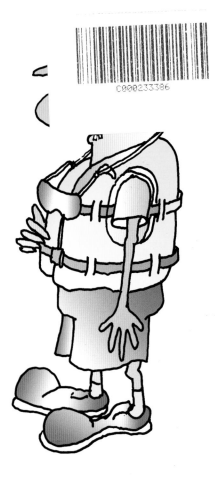

Published by Adlard Coles Nautical
an imprint of A & C Black Publishers Ltd
36 Soho Square, London W1D 3QY
www.adlardcoles.com

First edition published 2010

ISBN 978-1-4081-2677-6

A CIP catalogue record for this book is available from the British Library.

This book is produced using paper that is made from wood grown in managed, sustainable
forests. It is natural, renewable and recyclble. The logging and manufacturing processes
conform to the environmental regulations of the country of origin.

Printed and bound in China by South China Printing Co. Ltd.

the unofficial rules

of sailing

CARTOONS BY
Jim Crawford

ADLARD COLES NAUTICAL
LONDON

FOR JEANNINE. MY LOVER, MY PARTNER, MY FRIEND.

ALWAYS REMEMBER THE THREE Rs OF SAILING

RULE 2: (UN)FAIR SAILING

RULE 10: WHEN BOATS MEET ON OPPOSITE TACKS

HAIL FOR ROOM

RULE 17: SAILING A PROPER COURSE

RULE 18.2: GIVING MARK ROOM

RULE 20: ROOM TO TACK AT AN OBSTRUCTION

RULE 29.1: INDIVIDUAL RECALL

RULE 29.2: GENERAL RECALL

RULE 30.3: THE BLACK FLAG RULE

RULE 31.2: TOUCHING A MARK

RULE 40: PFDs REQUIRED (Y FLAG DISPLAYED)

RULE 41: OUTSIDE HELP

RULE 42.1: PROPULSION

RULE 42.2: PROHIBITED ACTIONS

THE INSIDE STARBOARD TACKER FINDS HIMSELF CONFLICTED BETWEEN RULES 41, 43 AND 41.2

MOVABLE BALLAST: RULE 51 APPLIES

RULE 60.2: THE RACE COMMITTEE...

RULE 60.3: THE PROTEST COMMITTEE...

THE PERILS OF THE PORTSMOUTH HANDICAP RULES

ANATOMY OF A MAIN SAIL

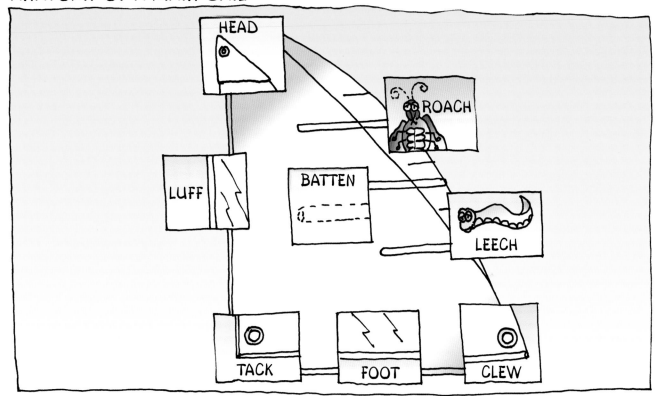

SHEETS

1 – MAIN SHEET

2 – JIB SHEET

3 – SHEETS TO THE WIND

MANOEUVRES

SAIL HAS RIGHT OF WAY OVER POWER

GYBING THE SPINNAKER

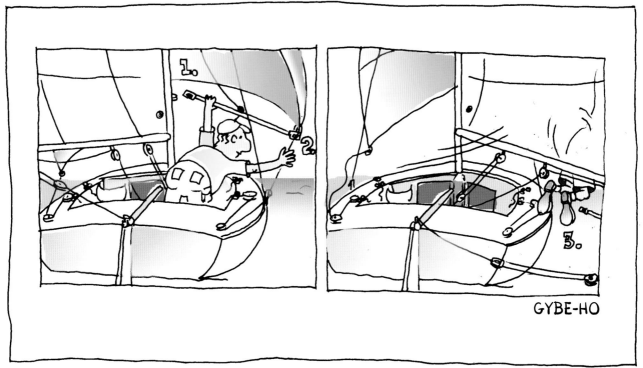

DOING THE HAND-GYBE

THROWING THE DUMMY TACK

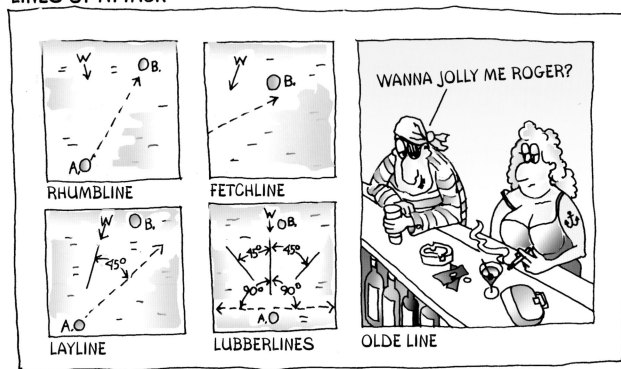

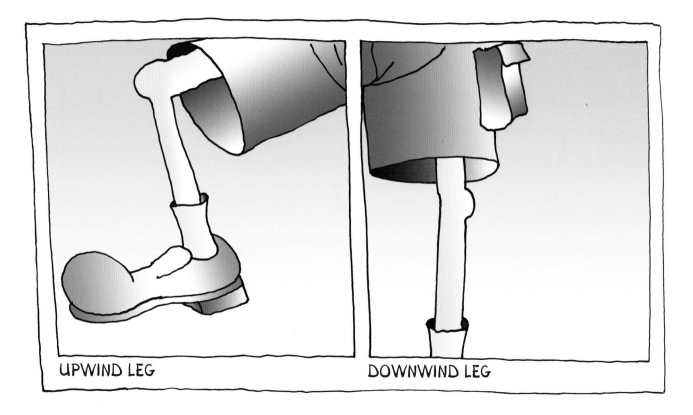

UPWIND LEG

DOWNWIND LEG

POOR TACTICS: OVER-PERFORMING THE ROLL-TACK

CRABBING TO WEATHER

RIGHT OF WAY

PRIVILEGED VESSEL

BURDENED VESSEL

NAUTICAL EQUIPMENT

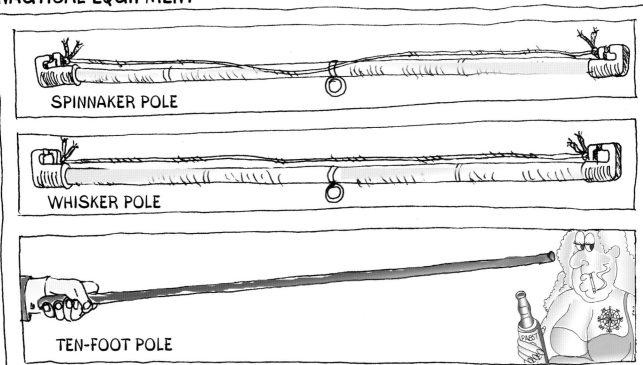

SPINNAKER POLE

WHISKER POLE

TEN-FOOT POLE

STANDING VS RUNNING RIGGING

BOAT PARTS

BOOM VANG   SPINNAKER GUY   OTHER GUY

BOAT PARTS

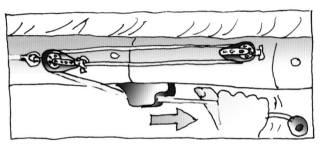

OUTHAUL

DOWNHAUL

OVERHAUL

KNOW THE WIND

ACTUAL WIND

APPARENT WIND

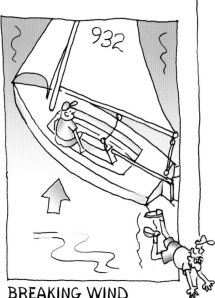

BREAKING WIND

EXECUTING THE HARD LUFF

CONFUSING KNOT

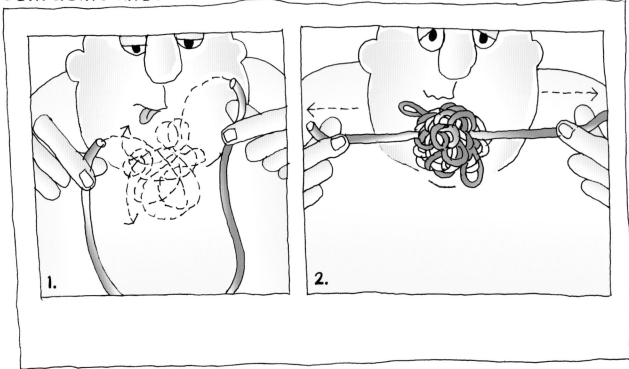

DECEPTIVELY SIMPLE KNOT

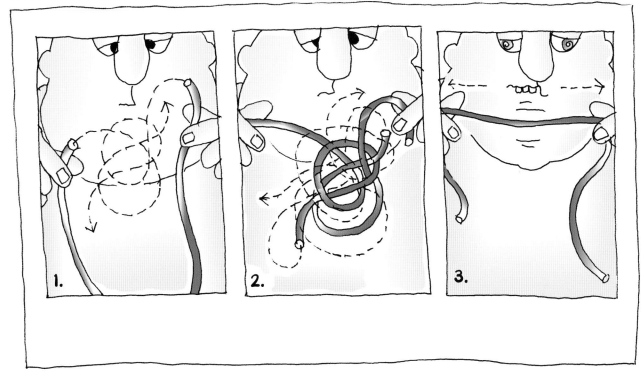

MARLINSPIKE EXPLAINED

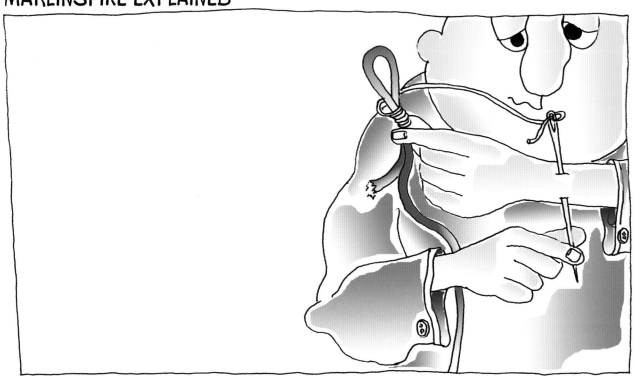

THE FAVOURED END

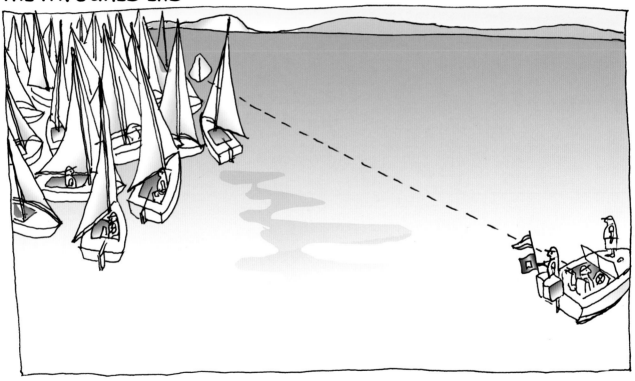

THE WAYS OF THE WIND

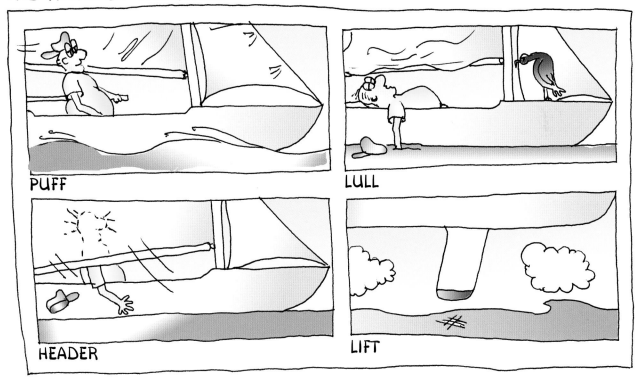

HEELING MOMENTS

HEELED

WELL HEELED

WHY WE DON'T WAX OUR DECKS

NOT TO BE CONFUSED

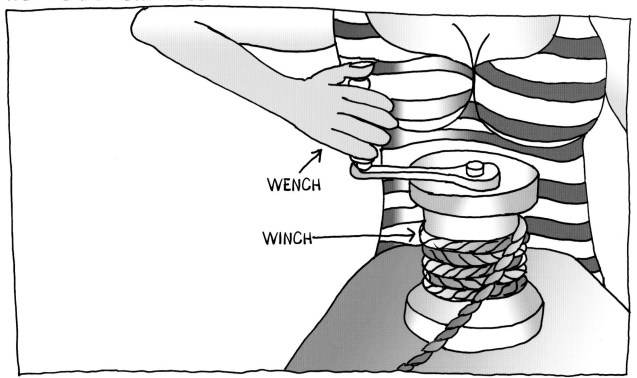

IMPROVED POINTING

THE STARBOARD TACK PARADE

SAILING THE BOAT ON HER EAR

AVOIDING 'BAD AIR'

BEAR OFF

WHY THEY CALL IT 'FOOTING'

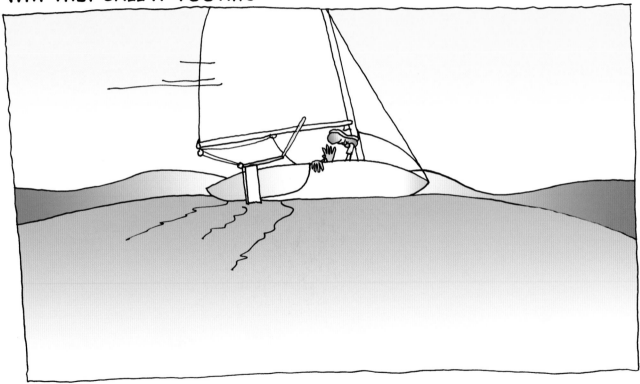

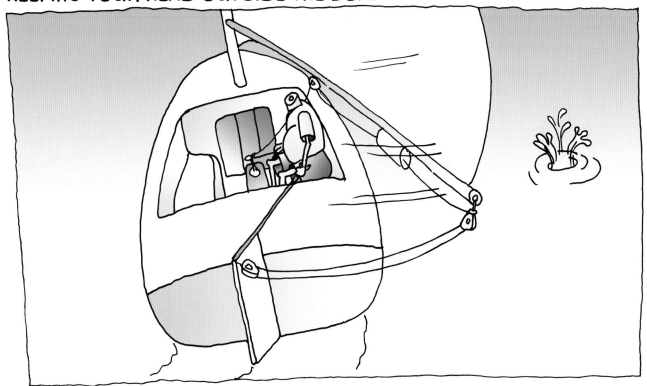

SAILING AFFLICTIONS

SAILOR'S EAR   SAILOR'S NOSE   SAILOR'S KNEE   SAILOR'S BLADDER

TWO MORE POINTS OF SAIL

CLOSE-HAULED

OVER-HAULED

MEASUREMENTS

JIB

JEB

FIGURING OUT THE BEAT

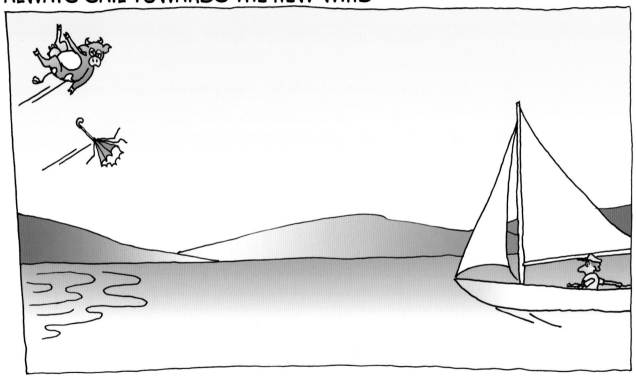

SAILING GEAR

SAIL

IN THE WIND

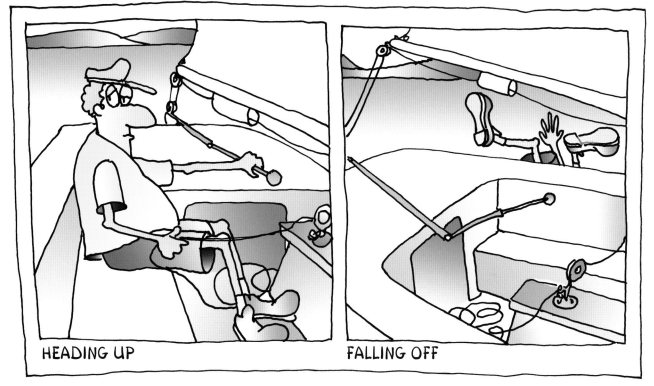

HEADING UP

FALLING OFF

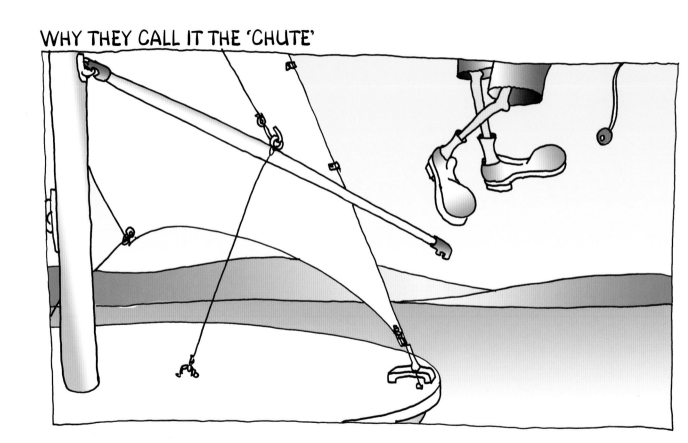

THE DOWNSIDE OF CROSS-SHEETING

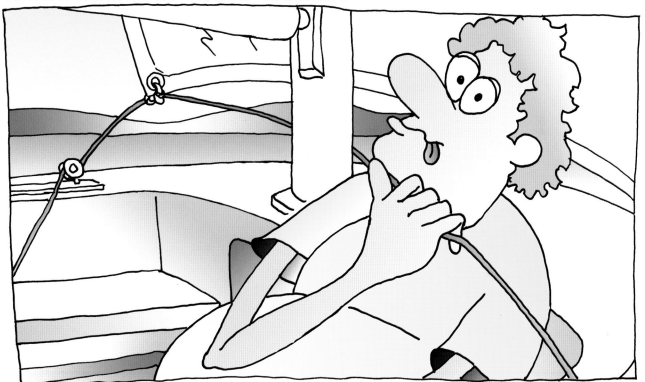

STARBOARD MEANS STARBOARD

HEAVING TO

BY THE LEE

HARD A-LEE

BROAD REACH

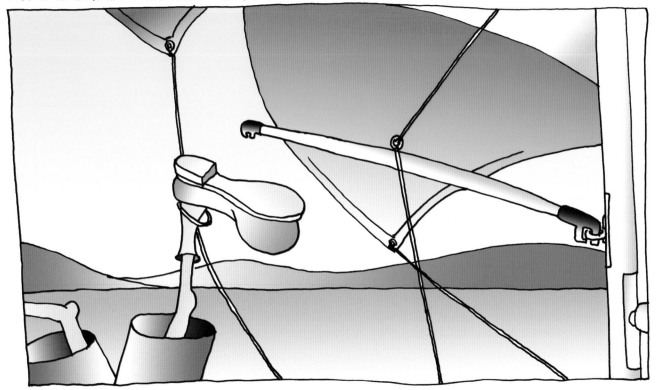

AN ILL-PREPARED SPINNAKER DROP

A GOOD STICK

BEWARE THE DREADED WIND SHADOW

THE DIP START

UNDER THE WEATHER HELM

POP QUIZ: WHO HAS THE RIGHT OF WAY?

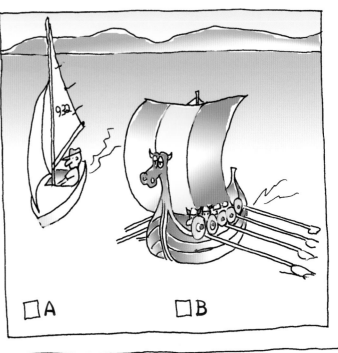

CONVERTING MILES INTO KNOTS

MILES →

MEANWHILE, ON THE COMMITTEE BOAT...

OTHER TITLES

Worse Things Happen at Sea
Jake Kavanagh
978-1-4081-1642-5

Jake Kavanagh turns his humorous eye to the scrapes people get into when let loose on the open water, highlighted with his hilarious cartoons.

Mike Peyton's Floating Assets
Mike Peyton
978-0-7136-8935-8

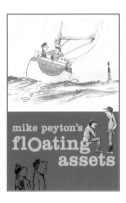

A wonderful collection of Mike Peyton's lighthearted and amusing recollections of time spent messing about in boats, all illustrated in his unique cartoon style. A perfect bunkside read for seafarers and landlubbers alike.

Foul Bottoms
John Quirk
978-1-4081-2269-3

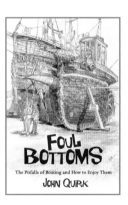

A witty collection of articles from *Classic Boat* magazine, illustrated with evocative cartoons, dwelling on the trials and tribulations people put themselves through when building, owning and sailing boats of all descriptions.

Yachting Monthly's Confessions
Yachtsmen Own Up to their Sailing Sins
978-1-4081-1639-5

A collection of embarrassing yachting faux pas which hundreds of humbled readers have owned up to in the pages of *Yachting Monthly,* accompanied by Mike Peyton's poignant cartoons.